COOKING FOR TWO

now you're cookin'

© 2007 Rebo International b.v., Lisse, The Netherlands

This title is a revision of title Cooking for Two that was published by Rebo Productions in 1998.

Recipes and photographs on pages 20-21, 24-25, 26-27, 40-41, 44-45, 52-53, 56-57, 58-59, 60-61, 62-63, 64-65, 66-67, 68-69, 90-91: © Ceres Verlag, Rudolf-August Oetker KG, Bielefeld, Germany

All other recipes and photographs: © Quadrillion Publishing Ltd, Godalming, Surrey

Design and layout: Minkowsky Graphics, Enkhuizen, The Netherlands

Typesetting: AdAm Studio, Prague, The Czech Republic

Cover design: Minkowsky Graphics, Enkhuizen, The Netherlands

Translation: Stephen Challacombe

Proofreading: Sarah Dunham

ISBN: 978-90-366-2236-3

now you're cookin'

COOKING
FOR TWO

THIS BOOK JUST MAKES YOU WANNA COOK

REBO
PUBLISHERS

Introduction

Planning and cooking a meal for two is a much more focused and in some ways more demanding occupation than catering for the family or even entertaining a group of guests. You are only too aware of the need to satisfy the tastes of your fellow diner while wanting to make sure you can share in that enjoyment.

In the case of a partner or close friend or relative, the challenge is to surprise and delight with your culinary creations – even if it's an everyday meal – given that they are likely to be familiar with your usual repertoire. But experimentation with innovatory concoctions can be a high-risk strategy, and you could all too easily lose the confidence of your companion in your cooking skills if you serve up a few disasters! The disappointing meals, rather unjustly, are often the ones that stick in the mind more than the successes.

If you are entertaining a sole guest who is less well acquainted with your track record in the kitchen, you are bound to be eager to impress. You will want to prepare something fail-safe but with an element of flair and creativity. The nature of the occasion will also have bearing on what you decide to cook. A leisurely lunch or dinner gives you lots of scope for producing more elaborate dishes, but a pre-film or theatre meal will have implications for advance preparation and cooking times.

The recipes in this special collection will give you the solutions you're looking for to all these culinary challenges. There are favorite and easy-to-prepare pasta and rice dishes which cannot fail to please any day of the week, together with exciting and sophisticated main courses for more formal occasions. Team these with the range of elegant starters and luxurious desserts on offer for a complete meal for two in memorable style. Some of the recipes are specially designed for preparation in the microwave, so that you can create delicious dishes for lunch or supper with the minimum of time and effort. So, put your worries behind you and let the good times roll!

Conversion tables

Measurements

teaspoons	tablespoons	cups	fluid ounces	milliliters
1				5
3	1	$\frac{1}{16}$	$\frac{1}{2}$	15
6	2	$\frac{1}{8}$	1	30
	4	$\frac{1}{4}$	2	60
	5 $\frac{1}{3}$	$\frac{1}{3}$	2 $\frac{1}{2}$	75
	6	$\frac{3}{8}$	3	90
	8	$\frac{1}{2}$	4	125
		$\frac{2}{3}$	5	150
		$\frac{3}{4}$	6	175
		1	8	237
		1 $\frac{1}{2}$	12	355
		2	16	473
		3	24	710
		4	32	946

Oven Temperatures

150 °C	300 °F
160 °C	325 °F
180 °C	350 °F
190 °C	375 °F
200 °C	400 °F
220 °C	425 °F
230 °C	450 °F

Method

Remove the heads and shells from the shrimp, but leave on the very ends of the tails. Wash, devein and pat dry. Place the oil and garlic in a microwave-proof bowl and cover with cling film. Cook in a microwave oven on HIGH for 1 minute.

Stir in the chilli sauce, wine, lemon juice and salt. Cook for 30 seconds on HIGH. Add the prawns, stir to mix and cook for 3–4 minutes on MEDIUM. Serve immediately, garnished with chilli flowers.

Chilli Shrimp

Ingredients

8 oz jumbo shrimp

1 tsp vegetable oil

1 clove garlic, crushed

1 tbsp chilli sauce (hot or sweet)

1 ½ tsp rice wine

1 ½ tsp lemon juice

Salt

Chilli flowers, to garnish (see Cook's tip)

Serving suggestion

Serve hot or cold with warm crusty bread.

Variations

If uncooked shrimp are not available, use cooked shrimp and reduce the cooking time by half. Use sherry in place of rice wine. Use curry sauce or paste in place of chilli sauce.

Cook's tip

To make chilli flowers, cut fresh chillies into thin strips beginning at the pointed end and cutting down to the stem end but without cutting completely through the stem. Rinse out the seeds and leave the chillies in iced water for several hours. The strips will open up and curl back like petals.

Method

In a bowl, mix the cheese with the chopped herbs and onion and shallot.

Mix in the capers, peppercorns and salt and pepper. Stir in the vinegar, lemon juice and olive oil. Mix well. Divide the cheese between 2 small ramekins, pushing it down well, then set in the refrigerator for about 2 hours.

Turn out onto serving plates just before serving and serve, garnished with fresh herb sprigs.

Ingredients

1 fresh goat cheese

2 tsp mixed fresh herbs, such as chives, parsley

and chervil

2 tsp finely chopped onion and shallot

6 capers

2 peppercorns

Salt and freshly ground pepper

A few drops of vinegar

A few drops of lemon juice

A few drops of olive oil

Fresh herb sprigs, to garnish

Herby Goat Cheese

Serving suggestion

Serve with a mixed salad tossed in vinaigrette and fresh

crusty bread.

Cook's tip

Use only fresh goat cheese – avoid the dry variety which

is often available, since it will crumble and will not blend

well with the herbs.

Method

Butter 2 individual ovenproof ramekins and break an egg into each one.

In a small bowl, stir the chopped tarragon and salt and pepper into the cream and mix well. Spoon 1 tbsp of the cream mixture over each egg, covering the egg completely. Place the ramekins on a baking sheet and cook in a preheated oven at 350 F for about 6–8 minutes, until set. Serve hot.

Ingredients

1 small knob of butter

2 large eggs

1–2 tsp chopped fresh tarragon

Salt and freshly ground black pepper

2 tbsp double cream

Eggs Baked in Tarragon Cream

starters & salads

Serving suggestions

Serve piping hot with buttered toast or crusty French bread.

Cook's tip

When cooking the eggs, check them during the cooking time to see how hard they have

become. If you cook them for 8 minutes, they will be very set. If you require a softer yolk,

cook them for a shorter time.

Method

Place the fish in a shallow dish and pour over a few spoonfuls of stock. Loosely cover the dish and cook in a microwave oven on HIGH for 4–5 minutes, or until the fish is cooked through. Flake the fish finely, discarding any bones. Set aside. Place the potatoes, onion, celery and remaining stock in a bowl. Cover loosely and cook on HIGH for about 10 minutes, stirring occasionally during cooking. Add the fish to the potato mixture, season with salt and pepper and stir in the lemon juice. Add the milk and stir to mix. Cover loosely and cook for a further 5 minutes on HIGH, stirring occasionally. Allow the soup to stand for about 2 minutes before serving. Garnish with the chopped hard-boiled egg and parsley and serve.

Ingredients

8 oz smoked haddock fillets, skinned

1 ½ cups hot fish or vegetable stock

4 oz potatoes, diced

1 medium onion, chopped

1 stick celery, finely chopped

Salt and freshly ground black pepper

1 ½ tsp lemon juice

1 ½ cups milk

1 hard-boiled egg, shelled and chopped

1 tbsp chopped fresh parsley

Cream of Smoked Haddock Soup

Serving suggestions

Serve with fresh crusty French bread or toast.

Variations

Use smoked cod in place of haddock. Use 1 leek in place of the onion. Use sweet potatoes in place of standard potatoes.

Method

Mix the basil with the French dressing in a small jug or bowl. Set aside.

Cook the pasta shapes in a large saucepan of lightly salted, boiling water for about 10 minutes, until tender. Rinse in cold water and drain well, shaking off any excess water. Place the pasta shapes in a bowl and toss with half the French dressing, mixing well to ensure that they are evenly coated. Set aside to cool. Slice enough of the tomatoes to arrange around the outside of a serving dish, then chop the remainder. Place the chopped tomatoes in another bowl and pour over the remaining French dressing. Place this in the center of a serving dish. Add the flaked tuna to the pasta shapes and toss together gently.

Pile the pasta shapes and tuna over the chopped tomatoes in the center of the dish. Arrange the tomato slices around the edge of the serving dish and chill well until required.

Tuna and Tomato Salad

Serving suggestion

Serve this salad as part of a summer lunch, with a crisp green salad and lots of French bread.

Ingredients

2 tsp chopped fresh basil

3 tbsp French dressing

6 oz pasta shapes of your choice

3 tomatoes

6 oz canned tuna, preferably in water or brine, drained and flaked

Variations

Add 1 tbsp halved, pitted black olives for a different flavor. Use canned salmon or crab in place of tuna. Use fresh parsley, chives or coriander in place of basil.

Method

Place the salmon in a small casserole dish with the bay leaf and 2 tbsp water. Cover and cook in a microwave oven for 4–6 minutes on HIGH, or until the fish flakes. Remove and discard the skin and bones and place the fish in a food processor or blender. Reserve the cooking liquid and discard the bay leaf.

Blend the fish with the soft cheese, tomato purée, dill, lemon juice, salt and Tabasco until smooth and well mixed. Add the reserved cooking liquid as necessary if the mixture is too thick. Spoon the salmon mixture into mounds on 2 small serving dishes and chill until firm. Before serving, spread 1 tbsp of mayonnaise carefully over each mound of salmon mousse.

Cut the slices of smoked salmon to size and press onto the mayonnaise carefully to cover the mousse completely. Leave at room temperature for about 30 minutes before serving.

Garnish with the slices of cucumber, lemon and dill sprigs.

Quick Salmon Mousse

Ingredients

8 oz salmon

1 bay leaf

2 oz low-fat soft cheese

¼ tsp tomato purée

1 tsp chopped fresh dill

1 ½ tsp lemon juice

Salt

A dash of Tabasco® sauce

2 tbsp mayonnaise

2 oz thinly sliced smoked salmon

Cucumber slices, lemon slices and fresh dill sprigs, to garnish

Serving suggestions

Serve with brown bread or melba toast.

Variations

Use trout fillets in place of salmon. Use fresh tarragon in place of dill.

17

Method

Heat the oil in a saucepan and fry the onion and garlic gently for about 2–3 minutes, until the onion is soft but not colored, stirring occasionally.

Stir in the potato, carrot and celery and fry for a further 3 minutes, stirring occasionally. Stir in the cabbage and tomatoes and cook for a further 5–6 minutes, stirring occasionally. Add the water or stock to the vegetables in the saucepan, then add the bouquet garni. Stir in the peas, kidney beans and pasta, cover and simmer gently for 10–15 minutes, or until the pasta is just tender, stirring occasionally. Remove and discard the bouquet garni, season with salt and pepper and ladle into individual serving bowls. Sprinkle generously with the grated Parmesan and serve.

Ingredients

1 tbsp olive oil

1 small onion, chopped

1 clove garlic, crushed

1 medium potato, scrubbed and diced

1 carrot, diced

1 stick celery, roughly chopped

3 oz cabbage, shredded

2 fresh or canned tomatoes, chopped

1 ¾ cups water or vegetable stock

1 bouquet garni

3 oz fresh or frozen peas, shelled

2 oz cooked red kidney beans

2 oz macaroni or any pasta shape

Freshly ground sea salt and black pepper, to taste

1 oz fresh Parmesan cheese, grated

Minestrone Soup

Variations

Use any vegetables of your choice in place of the carrots,

celery, potatoes and cabbage.

It is traditional for the soup to have peas and beans in it,

so do not substitute these.

Use wholewheat pasta for a change.

Cook's tip

If you prefer a thicker soup, stir 1 tbsp tomato purée into

the soup 5 minutes before serving.

starters & salads

Method

Wash the spinach leaves thoroughly and roughly chop. Place the spinach in a pan with the stock and bring to the boil. Season with pepper and nutmeg, then add the whole onion to the stock. Cover and simmer for about 35 minutes, stirring occasionally. Remove and discard the onion. Cool the soup slightly, then purée in a food processor or blender until smooth. In a small bowl, mix the butter and flour together to form a dough, then roll into small dumplings. Set aside.

Return the soup to the rinsed-out pan and bring gently to the boil, stirring occasionally. Add the dumplings and simmer for about 5 minutes, until cooked.

Stir in the cream and cheese and heat gently, stirring occasionally.

Ladle into soup bowls and serve, garnished with fresh herb sprigs.

Cream of Spinach Soup

Ingredients

14 oz fresh spinach leaves

1 ¾ cups vegetable stock

Freshly ground black pepper and grated nutmeg,

to taste

1 small onion

1 tsp butter

4 tsp plain flour

½ cup double cream

1 oz Roquefort cheese, crumbled

Fresh herb sprigs, to garnish

Serving suggestion

Serve with melba toast.

Variations

Use chard or green cabbage in place of spinach.
Use creme fraiche in place of cream. Use Stilton in place of Roquefort.

21

Method

In a large bowl, mix the beans and chick-peas together thoroughly. Set aside.

Place the sugar and wine vinegar in a small bowl together with the salt and pepper. Stir in the oil, mustard and basil. Whisk the vinegar mixture vigorously with a fork until it becomes thick. Pour the dressing over the beans and mix in thoroughly to coat the beans evenly. Refrigerate until ready to serve. Before serving, mix the onion rings and parsley into the bean salad, reserving a few onion rings for garnishing. Serve.

Ingredients

3 oz cooked red kidney beans

3 oz cooked black-eyed beans

3 oz cooked butter beans

2 oz cooked broad beans, shelled

4 oz cooked green beans, sliced

3 oz cooked chick-peas

1 tbsp brown sugar

¼ cup white wine vinegar

¼ tsp salt

A pinch of black pepper

¼ cup olive oil

¼ tsp dry mustard powder

¼ tsp dried basil

1 Spanish or red onion, thinly sliced into rings

1 tbsp chopped fresh parsley

Mixed Bean Salad

Variations

Stir 2 oz very small cauliflower or broccoli florets into the salad. Use walnut or hazelnut oil in place of olive oil. Use fresh chives or coriander in place of parsley.

Cook's tips

If you want to cook the dried beans yourself, soak them in separate bowls overnight and then bowl them rapidly in separate pans for at least 30 minutes, until they are completely tender. Rinse in cold water and drain well. Otherwise, use canned beans, drained and well rinsed.

Method

Place the tomatoes in a bowl and pour over boiling water, then plunge into cold water. Skin the tomatoes, cut in half and remove and discard the seeds. Slice the flesh into 8 segments. Melt the butter in a pan, add the onion, mushrooms and green pepper and cook until the onion is soft, stirring occasionally.

Add the stock to the pan and cook for a further 10 minutes. Add the tomatoes and cook for a further 2–3 minutes, stirring occasionally. Blend the cornflour with 2 tbsp water in a bowl. Stir the cornflour mixture into the vegetables and cook until thickened, stirring. Simmer for 3 minutes.Add the tomato purée, pepper and garlic salt, then stir in the cream. Serve, sprinkled with chopped parsley to garnish.

Ingredients

2 small tomatoes

1 tbsp butter

1 large onion, thinly sliced

2 oz cooked chantarelle mushrooms, sliced

1 large green pepper, seeded and sliced

4–6 tbsp vegetable stock

1 tbsp cornflour

1 tbsp tomato purée

Freshly ground black pepper and

garlic salt, to taste

1 tbsp double cream

Chopped fresh parsley, to garnish

Mediterranean-Style Vegetables

Serving suggestions

Serve with garlic bread or baked potatoes.

Variations

Use 1 red or yellow pepper in place of green. Use plum tomatoes in

place of standard tomatoes. Use 1–2 leeks in place of the onion.

Method

Heat the oil in a pan, add the onion, garlic, peppers, eggplant and zucchini and cook for 20 minutes, stirring occasionally. Add the tomato and tomato purée and season to taste with rosemary, thyme and salt and pepper. Simmer gently while you make the piccata. For the piccata, slice the lamb into pieces about 1 ½ oz each and flatten each piece slightly with the side of a meat cleaver.

Season with salt and pepper, then dust each piece of meat with flour. In a bowl, beat the egg and stir in the cheese. Coat each piece of meat all over with the egg mixture. Heat the oil in a frying pan, add the meat and cook over a low to medium heat until cooked through and golden brown all over, stirring occasionally. Halve and seed the remaining green pepper and place each half on a plate. Spoon the ratatouille into the pepper halves. Serve with the cooked hot meat alongside.

Lamb Piccata with Ratatouille

Ingredients

For the ratatouille

1 tbsp olive oil

1 small onion, thinly sliced

1 small clove garlic, thinly sliced

1 small red pepper, seeded and sliced

1 small green pepper, seeded and sliced

1 small eggplant, sliced

1 zucchini, sliced

1 tomato, skinned

1 ½ tsp tomato purée

Chopped fresh rosemary and thyme, to taste

Salt and freshly ground black pepper

For the piccata

8 oz boned loin of lamb

Salt and freshly ground black pepper

1 tbsp plain flour

1 medium egg

2 tsp grated Cheddar or mature Gouda

1 tbsp olive oil

1 green pepper

27

Method

Break the eggs into a bowl and beat in the milk and pepper. Heat the oil in a large non-stick frying pan and fry the green pepper until it is just soft, stirring occasionally. Stir in the tomatoes and the ham. Cook for 1 minute, stirring occasionally. Pour the egg mixture into the omelette pan over the vegetables. Stir the mixture briskly with a wooden spoon, until it begins to cook. As the egg begins to set, lift it slightly and tilt the pan to allow the uncooked egg to run underneath. When the egg on top is still slightly creamy, cut the omelette in half and slip each half onto a serving plate. Serve immediately.

Ingredients

6 medium eggs

¼ cup milk

Freshly ground black pepper

1 tbsp vegetable oil

2 oz chopped green pepper

4 tomatoes, skinned, seeded and roughly chopped

4 oz lean ham, cut into small dice

Ham and Green Pepper Omelette

Serving suggestion

Serve the omelette with a crisp leaf salad and French bread.

Variations

Use any selection of your favorite vegetables to vary this dish. Use
smoked ham for a change. Top the omelette with a little grated
cheese just before serving, if you like.

Method

Cut the eggplants in half lengthways. Score the cut surfaces lightly with a sharp knife, making sure that you do not break the skin. Brush lightly with 1 tsp of the oil and sprinkle with salt. Place the eggplants on a lightly greased baking sheet and cook in a preheated oven at 375°F for 15 minutes. Allow to cool slightly. Scoop the flesh carefully from each eggplant half, leaving about ¼ in around the edge, to form a shell. Chop the flesh. Fry the onion in a pan in the remaining oil until softened. Add the garlic and chopped eggplant flesh.

Cook for 2 minutes, then stir in the rice, mayonnaise, tuna, tomatoes, parsley, curry powder and salt and pepper to taste. Divide the rice mixture equally between the eggplant shells. Place the filled eggplants in an ovenproof dish and bake for 25 minutes. Serve hot, garnished with chopped fresh herbs.

Rice and Tuna Stuffed Eggplant

Ingredients

2 small eggplants

1 tbsp olive oil

Salt and freshly ground black pepper

½ small onion, finely chopped

1 small clove garlic, crushed

3 tbsp cooked brown or wild rice

1 ½ tsp mayonnaise

1 x 3 ½-oz can tuna, drained and flaked

2 tomatoes, skinned, seeded and chopped

½ tsp chopped fresh parsley

½ tsp curry powder

Chopped fresh herbs, to garnish

Serving suggestion

Serve with crusty French bread and a mixed leaf salad.

Variations

Use large zucchini in place of eggplants. Use creme fraiche in place of mayonnaise. Use canned salmon in place of tuna.

Cook's tip

A serrated spoon or grapefruit knife is useful for scooping out the eggplant flesh dish and bake for 25 minutes. Serve hot, garnished with chopped fresh herbs.

Method

Grease an ovenproof dish with the butter and spread the sliced potato over the base in layers. Mix the cream with the garlic, salt and pepper to taste and nutmeg. Pour the cream mixture over the potato, adding a little milk if the cream does not cover the potatoes, and cook gently in a pre-heated oven at 350°F for 1–1 ½ hours, until the potatoes are tender. Set the oven to its highest temperature, sprinkle over the grated cheese and cook until crisp and golden brown. Serve hot.

Ingredients

1 tbsp butter

2 lb 4 oz potatoes, peeled and thinly sliced

1 ¼ cups single cream

1 small clove garlic, crushed

Salt and freshly ground black pepper

A pinch of nutmeg

2 oz grated Gruyere cheese

Gratin Dauphinois

Serving suggestions

Serve with grilled mixed vegetables such as peppers, zucchinis and tomatoes or enjoy just on

its own with fresh crusty bread.

Variations

Add a layer of thinly sliced onion to the middle of the potatoes, for extra flavor. Use sweet

potatoes in place of standard potatoes. Use Cheddar or Emmenthal cheese in place of Gruyere.

Cook's tip

The relatively low cooking temperature of this dish is very important for a successful result. Do

not be tempted to increase the temperature of the oven.

light meals

Method

In a large, heavy-based frying pan, gently melt the butter, then increase the heat and cook the carrots, onions and bouquet garni. Shake the pan from time to time to prevent sticking. Once the vegetables begin to color reduce the heat,

cover and cook for 25–30 minutes, until the vegetables are tender, stirring occasionally. Meanwhile, blanch the bacon in a saucepan of boiling water, drain well and add to the carrot mixture. Sprinkle over the sugar, cinnamon and salt and pepper to taste, and continue to cook until very tender, stirring occasionally. Serve hot, garnished with chopped fresh herbs.

Ingredients

1 tbsp butter

1 lb carrots, thinly sliced into rounds

5 ½ oz onions, thinly sliced

1 bouquet garni

4 oz smoked bacon, diced

A pinch of sugar

A pinch of ground cinnamon

Salt and freshly ground black pepper

Chopped fresh herbs, to garnish

Fricassee de Carottes

light meals

Serving suggestions

Serve with garlic or herb-flavored bread, or with oven-baked

potatoes topped with cheese.

Variations

Use leeks in place of onions. Use ground ginger in place of

cinnamon.

Method

Wipe the chicken wings with absorbent kitchen paper and cut off and discard the tips. Place the wings in a shallow, non-metallic ovenproof dish.

Mix the remaining Ingredients together, except the garnish, pour over the chicken and allow to marinate, covered, for up to 24 hours in the refrigerator.

Allow the chicken to come to room temperature, then cook, uncovered, in a pre-heated oven at 400°F for about 30 minutes, basting once or twice, until cooked. Serve hot or cold, garnished with fresh herb sprigs.

Orange and Cardamom Chicken Wings

Ingredients

4 chicken wings

2 cloves garlic, crushed

Finely grated rind of 1 small orange

3 tbsp freshly squeezed orange juice

1 ½ tsp lemon juice

2 tbsp vegetable oil

Seeds from 5 cardamoms, crushed

Salt and freshly ground black pepper

Fresh herb sprigs, to garnish

Variations

Use lemon rind and juice or grapefruit in place of orange. Use cumin or coriander seeds in place of cardamom. Use lime juice in place of lemon juice.

Cook's tip

The chicken wings should be allowed to come to room temperature before cooking, otherwise they will take longer to cook.

Method

Lay the steaks on a board and rub both surfaces of each with the garlic and pepper. Place on a plate and refrigerate for 30 minutes. Heat the oil in a large frying pan and quickly fry the steaks for 1 minute on each side. Remove the steaks from the pan and set aside. Add the shallot, capers and mushrooms to the oil and meat juices in the frying pan. Cook for about 1 minute, stirring occasionally. Sprinkle the flour over the vegetables and fry gently until it begins to brown, stirring. Pour over the stock and stir well, adding the mustard, Worcestershire sauce, wine, lemon juice and thyme and rosemary as the sauce thickens, stirring continuously. Return the steaks to the sauce mixture along with the baby corn, peppers and tomatoes.

Simmer for 6–8 minutes, or until the steaks are cooked but still pink in the center, stirring occasionally. Serve at once.

Sweet Pepper Steaks

Ingredients

2 sirloin steaks, each weighing about 4 oz

1 clove garlic, crushed

Freshly ground black pepper

1 tbsp vegetable oil

1 shallot, finely chopped

2 tbsp capers

2 oz mushrooms, sliced

1 tbsp plain flour

¼ cup dark stock

2 tsp ready-made mustard

1 tsp Worcestershire sauce

4 tbsp white wine

1 tsp lemon juice

A pinch each of dried thyme and rosemary

4 baby corn cobs, cut in half lengthways

1 small green pepper, seeded and thinly sliced

1 small red pepper, seeded and thinly sliced

1 small yellow pepper, seeded and thinly sliced

2 tomatoes, skinned, seeded and cut into thin strips

Cook's tip

It is important to fry the steaks initially on both sides, since this helps to seal in the meat's juices.

Method

Slice the cucumber in half lengthways. Carefully remove and discard the seeds of the cucumber with a spoon and season the flesh with salt. Place the minced pork in a bowl with 1 chopped onion, the egg yolk and chopped parsley and mix well. Season the pork mixture to taste with pepper, marjoram and thyme. Divide the mixture equally between the 2 cucumber halves. Place the remaining onion, leek, celeriac and carrot in a microwave-proof dish with the butter. Place the stuffed cucumber halves on top of the vegetables. Pour over the wine, then place the lid on the dish and cook in a microwave oven on HIGH for 8–10 minutes, until the pork is cooked and tender. For the sauce, mix the creme fraiche with the hot stock in a bowl. Add the chopped dill and mix well.

Cover and cook the sauce in the microwave on HIGH for 3–4 minutes, stirring once. Adjust the seasoning of the sauce with pepper, marjoram and thyme.

serve the stuffed cucumber and vegetables with the sauce poured over. Garnish with fresh dill.

Stuffed Cucumber

Ingredients

1 cucumber

Salt

7 oz lean ground pork

2 onions, finely chopped

1 egg yolk

2 tbsp chopped fresh parsley

Freshly ground black pepper

Dried marjoram and thyme

1 leek, washed and thinly sliced

4 oz celeriac, cut into thin strips

1 carrot, cut into thin strips

2 tbsp butter

¼ cup white wine

3 tbsp creme fraiche

¾ cup hot vegetable stock

1 tbsp chopped fresh dill

Fresh dill, to garnish

Serving suggestions

Serve with fresh crusty bread and a mixed salad or crunchy homemade coleslaw.

Method

Remove the backbone from the chicken with poultry shears. Bend the legs backwards to break the ball and socket joints. Cut away some of the ribcage with a sharp knife. Flatten the chicken slightly with a meat mallet or rolling pin. Mix together the marinade Ingredients in a large, shallow dish or a large plastic bag. Add the chicken and turn to coat. If using a plastic bag, fasten securely and place in a dish to catch any drips. Refrigerate for at least 4 hours or overnight. Place the chicken on a grill pan and cook under a preheated low grill for about 30 minutes, turning and basting frequently with the marinade. Increase the heat and cook for a further 10 minutes, skin side up, to brown. Meanwhile, for the walnut sauce, place the garlic in a food processor and squeeze the bread to remove the water. Add the bread to the food processor along with the wine vinegar. With the machine running, pour the oil through the funnel in a thin, steady stream. Add the water if necessary to bring the sauce to coating consistency. Add salt and pepper to taste and stir in the walnuts by hand. When the chicken is cooked, place on a serving dish and pour over any remaining marinade. Serve with the walnut sauce. Garnish with lemon wedges and fresh parsley sprigs.

Ingredients

1 x 2 lb chicken, cut in half

Lemon wedges and freshly parsley sprigs, to garnish

A pinch of ground cumin

For the marinade

1 ½ tsp chopped fresh parsley

5 tbsp olive oil

1 tsp chopped fresh thyme

Juice and grated rind of 1 lemon

Salt and freshly ground black pepper

1 ½ tsp chopped fresh oregano or marjoram

A pinch of sugar

Marinated Chicken with Walnut Sauce

For the walnut sauce

1 clove garlic, roughly chopped

2 slices bread, crusts removed, soaked in water for 10 minutes

1 tbsp white wine vinegar

2–3 tbsp olive oil

1 tbsp water (optional)

Salt and freshly ground black pepper

1 ½ oz ground walnuts

Method

Sprinkle the fish with some lemon juice, place in a dish and set aside for 15 minutes. Place the onion in a pan with the capers and stock and bring to the boil. Cook for about 5 minutes. Blend the cornflour with 2 tbsp cold water in a bowl and stir the mixture into the stock. Add tomato purée, mustard, salt and pepper, paprika and lemon juice to taste. Slice the gherkins into strips and stir into the sauce. Bring to the boil, stirring continuously, until the sauce thickens slightly. Cut the fish into cubes, add to the sauce and simmer for 10–15 minutes, stirring occasionally, until cooked. Serve on a warmed serving dish or plates and sprinkle with the chopped parsley to garnish.

Ingredients

14 oz white fish fillets, such as cod or haddock

Lemon juice

1 large onion, thinly sliced

1 tsp capers

1 cup hot fish stock

1 tbsp cornflour

Tomato purée and mustard

Salt and freshly ground black pepper

Paprika

2 gherkins

Chopped fresh parsley, to garnish

Fish Stroganoff

Serving suggestion

Serve with rice or couscous and cooked fresh vegetables

such as broccoli and baby corn.

Variations

Use 2 leeks or 8 shallots in place of the onion.

Use monkfish or fresh tuna in place of cod or haddock.

Method

Place the sausage, ham, pepper, onion, garlic, chilli and oil in a large microwave-proof casserole dish or deep bowl. Stir to coat all the Ingredients in oil and cover the bowl loosely. Cook in a microwave oven on HIGH for 6–7 minutes, or until the onion and pepper are almost tender, stirring ccasionally.

Mix together the canned tomatoes, tomato purée and wine or lemon juice and add to the bowl. Add the marjoram, bay leaf, nutmeg and salt and pepper to taste and loosely cover the bowl. Cook for 2–3 minutes on HIGH, then stir in the prawns, tomato and rice. Re-cover the bowl and cook for a further 4 minutes on HIGH, or until all the Ingredients are hot, stirring once or twice. Remove and discard the bay leaf before serving. Serve, garnished with lemon slices.

Ingredients

4 oz spicy sausage, such as

Pepperoni or Merguez, skinned and diced

4 oz cooked ham, cubed

1 small green pepper, seeded and

cut into 1-inch pieces

1 small onion, roughly chopped

1 clove garlic, finely chopped

1 small fresh red or green chilli, seeded and finely

chopped

1 tbsp olive oil

5 ½ oz canned tomatoes

1 ½ tsp tomato purée

1 tbsp white wine or lemon juice

A pinch of chopped fresh marjoram

1 bay leaf

A pinch of grated nutmeg

Salt and freshly ground black pepper

2 oz cooked, shelled prawns

1 tomato, skinned, seeded and cut into

large pieces

3 oz cooked long-grain rice

Lemon slices, to garnish

Serving suggestion

Serve with crusty French bread and a mixed

leaf side salad.

Jambalaya

Variations

Use chicken in place of ham, cut into 1-inch pieces

and cooked with the onion and pepper.

Use salami or garlic sausage in place of

Pepperoni or Merguez.

Method

Melt half the butter and all the oil in a large frying pan over a moderate heat. When the foam begins to subside, brown the chicken, skin side down first. Pour off most of the fat from the pan and return the chicken to the pan. Pour the Calvados into the pan and warm over a gentle heat. Ignite with a match, then shake the pan gently until the flames subside. Pour over the stock and scrape up any browned chicken juices from the bottom of the pan. Set the chicken aside. Melt the remaining butter in a small saucepan. Cook the chopped apples, shallot, celery and thyme for about 10 minutes, or until soft but not brown, stirring occasionally. Spoon over the chicken and return the chicken pan to a high heat. Bring to the boil, then reduce the heat, cover and simmer for 50 minutes, stirring occasionally. When the chicken is cooked, beat the egg yolk and cream together in a bowl. With a whisk, gradually beat in some of the hot sauce. Pour the mixture back into a saucepan and cook over a low heat for 2–3 minutes, stirring constantly until the sauce thickens and coats the back of a spoon.

Season to taste.

Poulé Sauté Vallee D'Auge

Ingredients

2 tbsp butter

1 tbsp olive oil

4 chicken joints, two breasts or legs and 2 thighs or wings

2 tbsp Calvados

3 tbsp chicken stock

1 dessert apple, peeled, cored and coarsely chopped

1 shallot, finely chopped

1 stick celery, finely chopped

A pinch of dried thyme, crumbled

1 egg yolk, lightly beaten

3 tbsp double cream

Salt and freshly ground black pepper

Method

Rub the poussins inside and out with salt and pepper. Brush the skins with oil and push a wedge of lemon or lime and a bay leaf into the center of each one.

Roast the poussins on a baking tray, uncovered, in a preheated oven at 375°F for 45 minutes, or until just tender. Meanwhile, heat the 1 tbsp oil in a large frying pan and gently cook the onion and garlic until soft but not colored, stirring occasionally. Cut a slit into the skins of each tomato and plunge into boiling water for 30 seconds, then plunge into cold water. Using a sharp knife, carefully peel away the skins from the blanched tomatoes. Chop the tomatoes roughly, removing and discarding the seeds and cores. Add the chopped tomatoes to the cooked onion and garlic, and fry gently for a further 2 minutes. Add all the remaining Ingredients, except the garnish, and simmer for 10–15 minutes, or until the tomatoes have completely softened and the sauce has thickened slightly, stirring occasionally. Arrange the poussins on a serving dish and spoon a little of the sauce over each one. Serve hot with the remaining sauce in a separate jug. Garnish with lemon or lime wedges.

Ingredients

2 small poussins	5 tbsp chicken or vegetable stock
Salt and freshly ground black pepper	1 ½ tsp tomato purée
Olive oil, for brushing	1 small fresh green chilli, thinly sliced
2 small wedges of lime or lemon	½ small red pepper, cut into thin strips
2 bay leaves	½ small green pepper, cut into thin strips
1 tbsp olive oil	1 tbsp chopped blanched almonds
1 small onion, thinly sliced	1 ½ tsp pine kernels
1 small clove garlic, crushed	6 small black olives, stoned
8 oz tomatoes	1 ½ tsp raisins
5 tbsp red wine	Lemon or lime wedges, to garnish

Poussins Espagnole

Variations

Use 2 shallots in place of the onion. Use hazelnuts in place of almonds. Use sultanas in place of raisins.

Cook's tip

If the poussins start to brown too much during the cooking time, cover them with aluminium foil.

Method

Cut the zucchinis into 1 ½-inch slices. Cook the zucchinis in a pan of boiling salted water for 5 minutes. Drain well in a colander. Cut the cheese and salami into cubes. Mix with the creme fraiche, egg and pepper and grated nutmeg in a bowl. Add the zucchini slices and mix well. Place the mixture in a greased ovenproof dish and sprinkle with the breadcrumbs and chopped almonds.

Dot with a few knobs of butter. Cook in a preheated oven at 375°F for 25–30 minutes, until golden brown on top. Serve hot.

Ingredients

10 ½ oz zucchini

Salt

3 ½ oz Emmenthal cheese

3 ½ oz salami

1 cup creme fraiche

1 medium egg, beaten

Freshly ground black pepper and grated nutmeg, to taste

1 heaped tbsp fresh breadcrumbs

½ oz chopped blanched almonds

Butter, for dotting

Zucchini Soufflé Feodora

Serving suggestion

Serve with fresh crusty bread and a tomato, pepper and onion salad.

Variations

Use mushrooms in place of zucchinis. Use Gruyere or Cheddar cheese in place of Emmenthal. Use ham in place of salami.

main dishes

Method

In a bowl, mix the dill, mustard and lemon juice or wine together thoroughly.

Cut three slits, just piercing the skin, on both sides of the herring and lay on a grill pan. Spread half the mustard mixture equally over the exposed side of each fish, pushing some into the cuts. Spoon a little of the melted butter over each fish, then grill the fish under a preheated grill for 5–6 minutes.

Turn the fish over and spread with the remaining mustard and dill mixture. Spoon over the remaining melted butter and grill for a further 5–6 minutes.

Sprinkle the fish with a little salt and pepper before serving. Serve, garnished with lemon slices and fresh dill.

Grilled Herrings with Dill and Mustard

Ingredients

2 tbsp chopped fresh dill

3 tbsp mild mustard

1 tbsp lemon juice or white wine

2–4 fresh herrings, cleaned but heads and tails left on

1 tbsp butter, melted

Salt and freshly ground black pepper

Lemon slices and fresh dill, to garnish

Serving suggestion

Serve with new potatoes and fresh cooked vegetables such as cauliflower and green beans.

Variations

Use whole fresh mackerel in place of herrings.

Use fresh coriander or tarragon in place of dill.

Method

Thinly slice the beef. Heat the oil in a pan, add the beef and cook over a high heat until browned all over. Add the leeks to the pan together with the garlic, salt and pepper to taste and stock. Bring to the boil, then reduce the heat, cover and simmer for 35 minutes, stirring occasionally. Top and tail the beans, cut in half, then add to the pan with the dried herbs. Cook for 20 minutes, stirring occasionally. Add the tomatoes and cook for a further 5 minutes.

Add the cooked pasta and chopped parsley and cook until piping hot, stirring occasionally. Adjust the seasoning and serve, garnished with fresh herb sprigs.

Ingredients

10 ½ oz lean beef

1 tbsp vegetable oil

5 ½ oz leeks, thoroughly washed and sliced

1 clove garlic, crushed

Salt and freshly ground black pepper

1 ¾ cups beef or vegetable stock

10 ½ oz French beans

Beef and Vegetable Hotpot

1 tsp dried mixed herbs

9 oz tomatoes, skinned and chopped

2 oz cooked pasta shapes

1 tbsp chopped fresh parsley

Fresh herb sprigs, to garnish

Serving suggestion

Serve with baked or mashed potatoes.

Method

Sprinkle the fish with lemon juice and place in dish. Leave in the refrigerator for 24 hours, turning occasionally. Cut the avocado in half, remove the stone, then peel and slice the flesh into segments. Arrange the sole fillets and prepared vegetables together on a dish or platter. For the dressing, mix the lemon juice with the oil, garlic or celery salt and green peppercorns in a bowl. Season to taste with pepper and drizzle over the fish. Serve, garnished with lemon slices and fresh dill.

Ingredients

1 lb 2 oz small lemon sole fillets

6 tbsp lemon juice

1 avocado

2 red peppers, seeded and cut into small dice

2 spring onions, sliced

For the dressing

Juice of 1 lemon

3 tbsp corn oil

½ tsp garlic or celery salt

1 tbsp green peppercorns

Freshly ground black pepper

Lemon slices and fresh dill, to garnish

Marinated Lemon Sole with Avocado

main dishes

Serving suggestions

Serve with rice or baked potatoes and a mixed salad.

Variations

Use thin fillets or strips of plaice, haddock or cod in place of lemon sole. Use

1 ripe mango in place of avocado. Use lime juice in place of lemon juice.

Method

Cook the pasta in a large pan of salted boiling water with the oil added for 10–12 minutes, stirring from time to time to separate the strands, until just cooked or al dente. Strain the pasta in a colander, rinse with cold water and leave to drain. Melt the 1 tbsp butter in a pan, then pour into an ovenproof dish. Add the tagliatelle, toss to mix and keep it warm in a low oven. Heat the 2 tbsp butter in a pan, add the garlic, mushrooms and parsley and cook for about 5 minutes, stirring occasionally. Add some of the liquid from the mussels, cover and simmer for 10 minutes. Add the mussels and cook until piping hot, stirring occasionally. Season to taste with pepper and onion salt.

Spoon the mussels over the hot pasta and serve immediately.

Tagliatelle with Mussels

Ingredients

9 oz tagliatelle

1 tbsp olive oil

1 tbsp butter, plus 2 tbsp butter

1–2 cloves garlic, finely chopped

9 oz mushrooms, sliced

1 sprig of fresh parsley, chopped

14-oz can mussels, drained and the liquid reserved

Freshly ground black pepper

Onion salt

Serving suggestion

Serve with ciabatta and a mixed leaf salad.

Variations

Use cooked, shelled prawns in place of mussels.

Serve the mussel sauce with other cooked pasta such as spaghetti or fettuccine.

Method

Preheat a microwave browning dish in a microwave oven on HIGH for 4–6 minutes. Add the butter and minced meat to the dish with the garlic. Cook in the open dish on HIGH for 3–5 minutes, stirring once or twice. Stir the tomato purée into the mince with the wine and the chopped oregano or marjoram, salt and pepper and paprika to taste. Add the tomatoes. Stir once more, then cook, covered, on HIGH for 4–5 minutes, stirring occasionally. Mix the mince mixture and macaroni together. Grease a flat microwave-proof dish with butter, place the macaroni and mince mixture in it and top with the cheese. Cover the dish and cook on HIGH for 5–6 minutes. Sprinkle the cooked dish with chopped basil and serve immediately, garnished with fresh herb sprigs.

Ingredients

1 tbsp butter

7 oz pork and beef, mixed

1 clove garlic, thinly sliced

1 tbsp tomato purée

¼ cup red wine

Chopped fresh oregano or marjoram

Salt and freshly ground black pepper

Paprika

14-oz can peeled tomatoes

10 ½ oz macaroni, cooked until al dente

Neapolitan Macaroni Soufflé

Butter, for greasing

1 ¾ oz Mozzarella cheese, thinly sliced

2 leaves of fresh basil, chopped

Fresh herb sprigs, to garnish

Serving suggestion

Serve with fresh crusty bread and a dark leaf salad.

Method

Cook the macaroni in a large saucepan of lightly salted boiling water for 8–10 minutes, until just cooked or al dente. Drain well and set aside. In a bowl, mix the butter and quark to a creamy consistency, then add the cream and stir well. Stir in the grated Parmesan cheese and season with salt and pepper and paprika to taste. Mix the sauce and pasta together, then place in a greased ovenproof dish. Cook in a preheated oven at 425°F for 5–10 minutes until hot. Serve immediately.

Macaroni with Quark

Ingredients

9 oz macaroni

1–2 tbsp soft butter

9 oz quark (low-fat curd cheese)

½ cup double cream

1 ½ oz grated Parmesan cheese

Salt and freshly ground black pepper

Paprika

Method

Cook the spaghetti in a large pan of salted boiling water for about 10 minutes, until just cooked or al dente. Strain through a colander and rinse with cold water. Set aside to drain. Melt the butter in a pan and fry the bacon pieces until cooked, stirring occasionally. Stir in the crème fraîche, then add salt and pepper and nutmeg to taste. Add the spaghetti to the pan and stir to reheat it evenly. Stir in the chopped basil and sprinkle with the grated Parmesan just before serving. Serve, garnished with fresh basil sprigs.

Spaghetti in a Cream Sauce

Ingredients

7 oz spaghetti

1 tbsp butter

3 ½ oz streaky bacon, cut into dice

7 oz crème fraîche

Salt and freshly ground black pepper

Grated nutmeg

1 tsp chopped fresh basil

Grated Parmesan cheese, to serve

Fresh basil sprigs, to garnish

Serving suggestion

Serve with wedges of focaccia and a plum tomato and onion salad.

Variations

Use tagliatelle in place of spaghetti. Use smoked bacon in place of unsmoked bacon. Use fresh parsley or chives in place of basil.

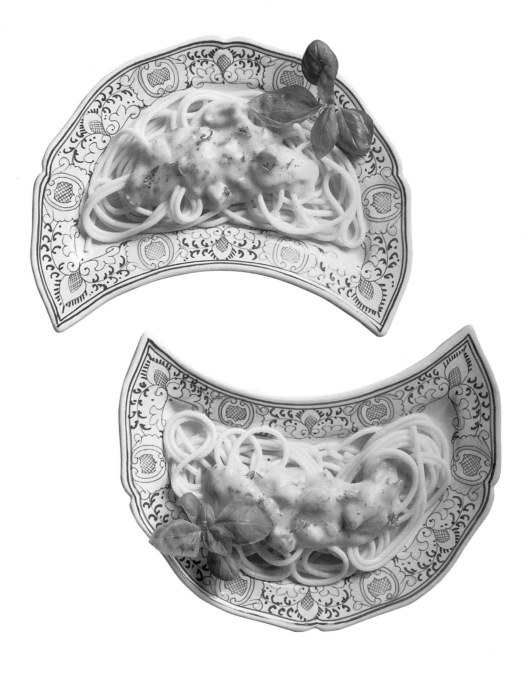

Method

Cut the pork into small cubes and set aside. Melt the butter in a pan and fry the bacon until browned all over, stirring occasionally. Add the pork and cook until browned all over, stirring occasionally. Add the onions and peppers and cook for about 10 minutes, stirring occasionally. Season to taste with salt and pepper, paprika and cayenne pepper, then stir in the tomato purée. Add the basil and lovage, then stir in the stock and tomatoes. Add the rice with 1 cup hot water and stir to mix. Bring to the boil, reduce the heat and simmer for a further 20 minutes, stirring occasionally, until the pork and rice are cooked and tender. Serve hot.

Multi-Colored Risotto with Pork

Ingredients

9 oz lean pork

1 tbsp butter

1 oz streaky bacon, cut into pieces

4 ½ oz onions, cut into quarters

1 small red pepper, seeded and sliced

1 small green pepper, seeded and sliced

Salt and freshly ground black pepper

Paprika

Cayenne pepper

1 tbsp tomato purée

1 tbsp chopped basil

1 tbsp chopped lovage

½ cup meat stock

9 oz tomatoes, skinned and cut into quarters

4 ½ oz long-grain white rice

Method

Shell the prawns, leaving 2 unshelled for a garnish. Set the prawns aside.

Place the prawn shells and wine in a saucepan and bring to the boil. Remove the pan from the heat and allow to cool completely before straining out the prawn shells and reserving the liquid. Heat the oil in a large frying pan or saucepan. Cook the onion and garlic gently without browning. Add the parsley and cook, stirring, for about 30 seconds. Add the rice to the pan and stir well to coat the grains with the oil. Add the reserved wine, tomatoes and tomato purée and just enough cold water to cover the rice. Season with salt and pepper to taste, then cook for about 20 minutes until all the water is absorbed and the rice is tender, stirring occasionally. When the rice is cooked, stir in the shelled prawns and cheese. Heat through gently until hot before piling into a serving dish. Garnish with the reserved prawns and the lemon slices, and serve immediately.

Prawn Risotto

Ingredients

8 oz unshelled prawns

½ cup white wine

1 tbsp olive oil

1 onion, chopped

1 clove garlic, chopped

1 tbsp chopped fresh parsley

3 oz brown rice

2 fresh tomatoes, chopped

½ tsp tomato purée

Salt and freshly ground black pepper

1 tbsp grated Parmesan cheese

Lemon slices, to garnish

Serving suggestion

Serve with fresh country-style bread and a mixed salad.

Method

Heat the oil and butter in a large frying pan and cook the onion and garlic over a gentle heat until soft and lightly browned, stirring occasionally.

Add the turkey cubes and cook until pale brown, stirring occasionally. Add the oregano and rice and cook for 1 minute until the rice is transparent, then add the tomato purée, stock and wine. Season with salt and pepper and stir well. Do not be tempted to stir the mixture again during cooking, since this will make the rice sticky. Cook over a very gentle heat for about 25–30 minutes, until all the stock has been absorbed but the rice still has a slight bite to it.

Lightly fork in the tomatoes, olives and chopped parsley, cook for 2 minutes, then serve sprinkled with Parmesan. Garnish with fresh parsley sprigs.

Ingredients

1 tbsp olive oil

2 tbsp butter

1 onion, thinly sliced

1 small clove garlic, crushed

8 oz boneless turkey breast, skinned and cut into ½-inch cubes

½ tsp dried oregano

4 oz Italian risotto rice

1 ½ tsp tomato purée

2 ½ cups chicken or turkey stock

A splash of white wine

Salt and freshly ground black pepper

3 tomatoes, skinned, seeded and chopped

6 stoned black olives, halved

Venetian Turkey

1 tbsp chopped fresh parsley

1 oz Parmesan cheese, grated

Fresh parsley sprigs, to garnish

Serving suggestion

Serve with crusty bread rolls and a crisp green salad.

Variations

Use a small can of tomatoes, drained and chopped, in
place of the fresh tomatoes. Use chicken in place of
turkey. Use 1 leek in place of the onion.

Method

Mix the single and double creams together in a small saucepan and stir in the sugar. Cook over a low heat until the cream begins to bubble and the sugar has melted. Stir in the grated lemon rind and allow the mixture to cool in the saucepan. Break the cake into fine crumbs and divide equally between 2 individual serving dishes. Stir the brandy into the cream mixture together with the lemon juice. Pour the cream mixture over the cake crumbs and refrigerate for 30 minutes, or until the cream has thickened. Sprinkle the toasted almonds over the top of the cream before serving. Serve immediately.

Lemon Brandy Cream

Ingredients

¾ cup single cream

¾ cup double cream

3 tbsp soft brown sugar

Finely grated rind and juice of 1 large lemon

1 ½ oz sponge cake

1 tbsp brandy

½ oz toasted flaked almonds

Serving suggestion

Serve with crisp almond biscuits and slices of fresh fruit.

Variations

Use the finely grated rind and juice of 1 small orange in place of the lemon and Cointreau in place of the brandy. Use ginger or chocolate cake in place of sponge cake.

Method

Place the cream cheese in a large bowl with 2 tbsp) of the cream. Whisk with an electric mixer until the mixture is light and fluffy. Mix in 1 ½ oz of the icing sugar and the cinnamon, stirring until all the Ingredients are well blended. Whip the remaining cream in another bowl until it forms soft peaks.

Fold the cream into the cheese mixture with a metal spoon. Line 2 individual Coeur à la Creme molds with dampened muslin, extending the fabric beyond the edges of the molds. Spoon the cheese mixture into the molds and spread out evenly, pressing down well to remove any air bubbles. Fold the overlapping edges of the muslin over the top of the mixture and refrigerate the molds on a rack placed over a tray to drain for at least 8 hours. Purée the raspberries in a food processor or liquidizer and press through a nylon sieve to remove all the seeds.Blend the remaining icing sugar into the fruit purée to sweeten. Carefully remove the muslin from the cream cheese hearts, and place each one on a serving dish. Spoon a little of the raspberry sauce over each heart and serve the remainder separately.

Cinnamon Coeur à la Crème
with Raspberry Sauce

Serving suggestion

Serve with a little extra whipped cream and crystallized rose petals for a special occasion.

Ingredients

4 oz cream cheese

1 cup whipping cream

2 oz icing sugar, sifted

1 tsp ground cinnamon

4 oz fresh raspberries

Cook's tip

It is important to use proper Coeur à la Crème molds since these have small holes in the base which allow any excess liquid to drain away during the chilling time.

Method

Halve the 3 passion fruits and scoop out all the flesh into a bowl.

Add the yogurt and egg yolk to the passion fruit flesh and mix together thoroughly.

Pour the passion fruit mixture into a shallow freezerproof container and freeze for about 1 hour, until partially set. Break up the ice crystals in the partially set passion fruit mixture using a fork, and mix well until a smooth slush is formed. Return the yogurt ice to the freezer and freeze until completely firm. To serve, remove the yogurt ice from the freezer for 10 minutes, then pile scoops into stemmed glasses. Serve with the passion fruit flesh poured over each portion, for decoration.

Passion Fruit Yogurt Ice

Ingredients

3 passion fruits

¾ cup plain yogurt

1 egg yolk

1 passion fruit, halved and the flesh

scooped out

and reserved, to decorate

Serving suggestions

Serve with wafer biscuits or sponge fingers.

Variations

Add 1 tbsp brandy to the yogurt ice mixture before freezing. Use fromage frais in place of yogurt.

Cook's tip

This yogurt ice goes extremely hard when frozen, so it is important to remember to remove it from the freezer 10 minutes before serving. Make double the recipe and keep half in the freezer for another time.

Method

Place the butter, sugar and lemon juice in a frying pan. Cook over a low heat, stirring continuously, until the butter has melted and the sugar has dissolved.

Peel the bananas and cut in half lengthways. Add these to the butter and sugar liquid in the pan and fry gently for a few minutes, basting well with the liquid. Add the brandy directly to the frying pan and cook for a second or two to warm the brandy through. Ignite the brandy carefully and allow the flames to die down before serving the bananas. Serve with the juices poured over and decorate with lemon slices.

Brandy Bananas

Ingredients

2 tbsp butter

1 tbsp soft brown sugar

1 tbsp lemon juice

2 bananas

2 tbsp brandy

Lemon slices, to decorate

Variations

Use Cointreau in place of brandy. Use lime or orange juice in place of lemon juice.

Cook's tip

If you have difficulty igniting the brandy, warm a little extra brandy separately in a pan and ignite it before you pour it over the bananas. Great care must be taken when using brandy to flambé a dessert.

Serving suggestion

Serve with a dollop of whipped cream.

Method

In a bowl, beat together the egg yolks with the sugar. Add the cherry juice and beat together thoroughly. Place the bowl over a pan of boiling water and cook, beating continuously. After a few minutes, the mixture will thicken and increase in volume. Remove from the heat and continue beating until cooled.

Spoon into individual dishes and serve with the whole cherries alongside.

Cherry Zabaglione

Ingredients

4 egg yolks

4 tsp sugar

1 tbsp cherry juice

10 whole cherries

Serving suggestions

Serve with almond or coconut cookies or a fresh fruit salad.

Variations

Use other fruit and juice such as peach slices and juice or grapes and juice in place of cherries. Use fresh strawberries and fruit liqueur in place of cherries and juice.

Cook's tip

To decorate the dessert, dip a fork in the cherry juice and drizzle the juice over the zabaglione.

Method

Cut each fig into quarters using a sharp knife and taking care not to cut right down through the base of the fruit. Ease the 4 sections of each fig outwards to form a flower shape. Place the ground almonds, orange juice and chopped apricots in a small bowl and mix together thoroughly. Divide the mixture in half and press into the center of each fig. For the sauce, mix the yogurt with the orange rind and thin it down with a little water or orange juice. Spoon a small pool of the sauce onto each of 2 plates and set a stuffed fig in the center of each pool. Decorate with additional wedges of fig and the mint or strawberry leaves. Serve immediately.

Almond-Stuffed Figs

Ingredients

2 large ripe figs

2 tbsp ground almonds

1 tbsp orange juice

1 tbsp finely chopped, ready-to-eat dried apricots

2 tbsp plain yogurt

Finely grated rind of ½ small orange

Wedges of figs and mint, or strawberry leaves,

to decorate

Serving suggestions

Serve with amaretti biscuits or sponge fingers

Variations

Use peach halves in place of figs. Use ground hazelnuts in place of almonds. Use dried pears or peaches in place of apricots.

Method

Using a potato peeler or very sharp knife, carefully pare the peel only away from the oranges. Cut the peel into very thin strips, removing and discarding any pith. Place the orange peel strips in a small bowl and cover with 2 tbsp boiling water. Allow to stand for 20 minutes, then drain. Carefully peel the pith from the oranges with a serrated-edged knife. Cut the oranges horizontally into slices about ¼-inch thick. Reserve any juice which spills in a small jug. Place the orange juice, ¾ cup water and sugar in a small saucepan and heat gently, stirring continuously, until the sugar has dissolved. Increase the heat and bring the sugar syrup to the boil, boiling rapidly until it turns a pale gold color. Remove the caramel from the heat and quickly stir in the boiling water. Add the orange rind to the sugar syrup along with the Cointreau and set aside to cool completely. Arrange the orange slices in a serving dish and pour over the cooled syrup. Chill for several hours or overnight before serving.

Caramel Oranges

Ingredients

2 large oranges

5 oz granulated sugar

2 tbsp boiling water

1 tbsp Cointreau

Variations

Use grapefruit (pink or red) in place of oranges.

Use brandy or sherry in place of Cointreau.

Serving suggestion

Serve with a dollop of crème fraîche or whipped cream.

Cook's tip

Take care not to overcook the sugar syrup, or it will burn and spoil the flavor.

Method

In a bowl, lightly whip the cream with the sugar, then mix in the ginger syrup. Set aside. Soak the gelatin in cold water for about 10 minutes, then dissolve in the orange juice in a pan over a gentle heat. Set aside to cool, then fold in the cream mixture. Grate the nuts and finely chop the stem ginger. Add the nuts and stem ginger to the cream and fold in to mix. Divide the mixture evenly between 2 individual damp jelly molds and chill in the refrigerator for at least 4 hours, until set. Meanwhile, remove and discard the peel and pith from the oranges, then thinly slice the flesh. Peel the mandarin, then remove the membranes from the segments and arrange with the slices of orange on 2 dessert plates. Turn the jellies out on top of the orange slices and serve, decorated with chopped orange rind and mint sprigs.

Ingredients

½ cup whipping cream

5 tsp sugar

½ tsp ginger syrup

2 sheets of white gelatin   1 blood orange

¼ cup orange juice   1 orange

1 oz brazil nuts   1 mandarin

1 piece of preserved stem ginger   Chopped orange rind and fresh mint sprigs, to decorate

Citrus Fruits in Ginger Cream Jelly

Serving suggestions

Serve with sponge finger biscuits or chocolate wafers.

Variations

Use pink or red grapefruit in place of the blood orange. Use hazelnuts or almonds in place of brazil nuts.

desserts

Method

For the filling, set aside a few strawberries for decoration. Purée the remaining strawberries in a food processor or blender until smooth.

In a bowl, mix the quark and sugar together, then add the lemon juice.

In a separate bowl, whip the cream until stiff, then fold in the quark mixture followed by the puréed strawberries, mixing well. Set aside. For the crepes, beat the egg yolks with the lemon rind and sugar in a bowl until creamy.

In a separate bowl, whisk the egg whites until stiff, then fold into the lemon mixture. Sift the cornflour over the top of the mixture and fold in.

Melt the butter in a large sauté or omelette pan and pour in half the egg mixture. Cover the pan and cook over a gentle heat until golden brown.

Spread half the filling over the crepe and fold over. Place on a plate and keep warm. Cook the second crepe in the same way. Serve the crepes decorated with the reserved strawberries and the fresh herb sprigs or strawberry leaves.

Crepes with Quark
and Strawberry Filling

Ingredients

For the filling

9 oz strawberries

9 oz quark (low-fat curd cheese)

1 oz sugar

1 tbsp lemon juice

½ cup whipping cream

For the crepes

3 medium eggs, separated

Finely grated rind of ½ lemon

1 oz sugar

1 tbsp cornflour

2 tbsp butter

Fresh herb sprigs or strawberry leaves, to decorate

Serving suggestions

Serve with a dollop of thick cream, Greek yogurt or crème fraîche.

Method

Separate the eggs and beat the yolk and sugar until it starts to foam.

Add the semolina, lemon juice and quark while stirring.

Beat the egg whites until firm and fold gently into the quark mixture.

Drain the morello well and fold in gently. Pour the mixture into greased soufflé forms.

Place in an oven at 400 °F and bake for 35 minutes. Serve the soufflé with a vanilla sauce.

Ingredients

3 eggs (medium size)

½ cup sugar

⅓ cup semolina

2 tbs lemon juice

1 lb lean quark

1 lb pitted morellos

Quark Soufflé with Morello

Method

Place the cranberries and the granulated sugar in a small, heavy-based pan.

Cook the cranberries slowly over a moderate heat until they soften and the juice begins to run. Set the cranberries aside to cool completely. Whisk the egg white in a bowl until stiff but not dry. Gradually whisk in the powdered sugar, whisking well between additions, until the egg white is smooth and glossy and forms stiff peaks. In a separate bowl, whip the cream until it is thick, then fold into the yogurt in a bowl. Fold the egg whites carefully into the cream and yogurt mixture. Stir in the cooked, cooled cranberries and the chopped mint. Do not over mix, since the dessert should look marbled. Spoon into individual serving dishes and serve, decorated with fresh mint sprigs.

Cranberry Snow with Mint

Ingredients

1 oz fresh or frozen cranberries

½ oz granulated sugar

1 egg white

1 oz powdered sugar

5 tbsp whipping cream

5 tbsp plain yogurt

1 tbsp chopped fresh mint

Fresh mint sprigs, to decorate

Serving suggestions

Serve with crisp biscuits or wafers.

Variations

Any kind of soft fruit can be used in place of cranberries. If you use blackcurrants, substitute blackcurrant leaves for the fresh mint, and if you use gooseberries, try combining them with elderflowers for a refreshing change.

Index